To Be Human Is To Be A Conversation

To Be Human Is To Be A Conversation

To Be Human Is To Be A Conversation

To Be Human Is To Be A Conversation

To Be Human Is To Be A Conversation

To Be Human Is To Be A Conversation

To Be Human Is To Be A Conversation

To Be Human Is To Be A Conversation

To Be Human Is To Be A Conversation

To Be Human Is To Be A Conversation

To Be Human Is To Be A Conversation

To Be Human Is To Be A Conversation

To Be Human Is To Be A Conversation

To Be Human Is To Be A Conversation

To Be Human Is To Be A Conversation

To Be Human Is To Be A Conversation

To Be Human Is To Be A Conversation

To Be Human Is To Be A Conversation

To Be Human Is To Be A Conversation

by Andrea Rexilius

RESCUE +PRESS

Rescue Press, Milwaukee 53212

Copyright © 2011 by Andrea Rexilius

Printed in the United States of America

www.rescue-press.org

Cover design by Skye McNeill
Book design by Rescue Press
First Edition

ISBN: 978-0-9844889-3-3
Library of Congress: 2011922031

To Be Human Is To Be A Conversation

Deconstruction of the Organ

Attempting Embrace: A Crisis in Form(ing)

Sister Sutures

Deconstruction of the Organ

Deconstruction of the Organ

"Each day that dawns is conclusive, as is each gesture spread
through daily living."
—Nicole Brossard, *Surfaces of Sense*

"The geometry of a gesture elaborates that of the framework."
—Anne-Marie Albiach, *Mezza Voce*

"Translating is more like wrenching a soul from its body
and luring it into a different one. It means killing."
—Rosmarie Waldrop, *Dissonance (if you are interested)*

Please describe the literal appearance of the organ in as much detail as possible.

My sister's name is Andrea Herzog. She is my only sibling. She is Hungarian. She moved to America when she was ten. I was eleven at the time. I met her when I returned home from visiting my mother in California. My father and I lived in Illinois. I returned home and another girl was wearing my clothes and sleeping in my room. We shared a bed for one year. My sister went to school with me and because she could not speak English, we shared a desk. She followed me to the bathroom and held onto my arm when we went outside for recess. My friends didn't like her very much. For one year she became my only friend. She learned English, but before that we communicated with our faces. We became telepathic. I learned to translate Hungarian without being able to speak, read, or comprehend it. My sister's mother's name is Agnes. My mother's name is Myra. My father's name is Jack. I don't know my sister's father's name. My sister's mother and my mother have the same birthday, January 5. My birthday is January 23. In Hungary name days are celebrated in place of birthdays. The name day for *Andrea* is January 23. This is how my sister and I came to be twins.

Are there any tastes or smells associated with the organ?

Transforms the figure, emotion. They felt something. They indulge as a result of repeated colonization. They make armies. They decide they are as small as ants. It happens on the cellular level. It happens as a result of frustration. Like *daffodils in the middle of the Pacific.* What they wanted most to see things they had never seen before. When they were people they felt relief. Consumption that begins bright and stimulating. Cyanide, benzene, chromium. They couldn't sleep. It was impossible for them to choose whether or not to be savage.

How does hearing the organ affect your body (your breathing, your heart rate, the degree to which you are "inside" or "outside" your body)? Are there certain ranges of sound produced by the organ that affect you more than others?

"The passage which the air follows partly through the nose and partly through the mouth, is the only one which man employs to pronounce the letter *a*; that is, the *a*. Though the tongue and lips do what they may, this will never prevent the air which streams out of the trachea from pronouncing the letter *a*, in this cavity *a*. Moreover, the letter *u*, is formed at the same place with the aid of the lips which are constricted and somewhat protruded. The more the lips are protruded the better the letter *u* is pronounced by them."

Please describe two scenes in detail in which you touched, played, moved, or otherwise interacted with the organ.

"Like disgust, [shame] operates only after interest or enjoyment has been activated, and inhibits one or the other or both. The innate activator of shame is the incomplete reduction of interest or joy. Hence any barrier to further exploration which partially reduces interest. . . will activate the lowering of the head and eyes in shame and reduce further exploration or self-exposure. . . Such a barrier might be because one is suddenly looked at by one who is strange, or because one wishes to look at or commune with another person but cannot because he is strange, or one expected him to be familiar but he suddenly appears unfamiliar, or one started to smile but found one was smiling at a stranger."

Please describe your hands. One-two paragraphs per hand.

In high school my sister and I were in a band called *Puritan Plainstyle*. She played the organ and I played the wind-up bird and victrola.

Please describe any tools and techniques you might use to destroy/dismantle the organ.

Impersonality; extraordinary rapidity of movement; a fugue.

Have you ever had a dream involving the organ?

In my dream I create a project called "Deconstruction of the Organ" in which I take the organ to the mountains, place it in an open field and gently and violently demolish it. I save sections of it to reconstruct into smaller instruments. I peel back layers of the organ to find the instrument within the instrument, the language within its language. In the dream I film the destruction of the organ. I film images of my back muscles tensing up, of the fluctuation of veins in my neck, of the tiniest movements of the wrist. I record the final song of the organ, the sound of the drills and hatchets and nail files and scissors I play it with. Harry Partch is in the dream. Mary Rowlandson is in the dream off in the distance. She is talking to Emily Dickinson. They eat a loaf of bread. My sister is there too.

First Residue

What is the relationship between the text and the body in your writing?

What is the relationship between the text and the body in your writing?

What is the relationship between the text and the body in your writing?

What is the relationship between the text and the body in your writing?

What is the relationship between the text and the body in your writing?

Interview   On   Sisterhood

What kinds of (physiological/psychological) responses does hearing, reading, saying, or writing the word "sister" create in you?

Do you respond differently to the word depending on whether or not it is spoken or written by another person or by yourself?

Can you list/map/describe these responses?

As A

Of A

In A

Essay   On   Sisterhood

A sister is an echo chamber. She is a nun, but the naked kind. Having religion is having a sister to speak in tongues with. You take a shower with your sister, and teach her to bathe her battlefield. She tells you what a country is, or what it means to divide. A sister is like war. She mimics you and you mock her. She will take your name out from under you. She will take your clothes and your culture. She will stand next to you in photographs, her face and your face exposed. A sister's breasts develop and her blood touches you. Your sister's brain makes a bridge against you. Your sister burns you down. My sister brings her palms up into the air, like this. She answers and her answers accumulate.

As A

Of A

In A

Essay   On   Sisterhood

One unifies by splitting the beginning of the other.

In a grove trees grow without genitals.

Born of a single root, each sibling is the self across distance.

Difference after all, is situational.

Based on coordinates, a vantage point.

Two eggs perched high in the nest cry out they have seen

ground between them, have gripped it with their head.

Like the first time you learned your own name. Noise of an individual sound moved in a strand; a stratum composing you.

Self composed of these branches.

A name being one form of self.

A namesis.

A person who rivals one's own emphasis on erasure.

When the bird returns to its nest a new thing

is born in place;

a new language inhabiting the gesticulation.

Memory a second form. The residue. Or resistant, residual I.

The very idea of *landscape* implies separation and observation.

The very idea of *body* implies separation and observation.

This is why I believe all fortresses are really nets. The pupil of the eye is an example. Light weaves into it from all around and gripping tendrils turn on their stalks into recognizable images. The body lunges forth, moveable, but it is the eye or net that accumulates, gorged on landscape. The eye knows it was what it saw once. To see things is to place your teeth on top of them. To create a building from the soldered pieces. An accumulation of meaning as it is defined by objects in the world. Now stuck in the eye's needle, needing things like a beak.

To talk is to touch; a simple noun.

Weighing the root beneath her. A liminal pause. Mouth gorged open in ground, a landscape. Where she has placed words there. Has planted silent speech. Hear how trees beckon it forward in silt. Trees rustling rusted bodies into breath. She has bundled them in bunches to burn.

Communist   Gesture

I do not know the day she arrived. I cannot mention the details because you will think them symbolic. You will not understand which things aren't metaphors. You will not believe me.

Our crime is what we are guilty of. A poverty of human blood. We reached across the median. Our crime is that sequence we were calling borderline. Our crime is she began to grow in my skin. A con artist. A mammal. A flower at the back of my skull.

Why does a flower exist?

What does it mean to be bilingual?

To be specific here is to be absurd.
There is this gap. A wolf goes a month or 40 days. The bitch nine weeks.

Long walks in the snow.

I read the noblest animals are the longest in gestation. Interior of
her body an image of tenderness. A chair in which an open field is
carried on certain occasions. Fear when night begins again. She gives
birth to me.

She gives birth to me as her hungry thing.

I see strata and reflection.
                    A parallel self returning.
                                        The other existing as
the condition I am in.

A month or 40 days. Complication of ulterior things.

What is the beauty of the geographer?

Who am I when I sleep?

I cannot find her on this land.

Complication of ulterior things.

She understood hibernation as a state not unlike the snow storm.
Everything matted down in white.

Our crime overlaps, merges. Is cited in this place as proof. A measure in quotation marks. *Well*, to emphasize. The image appears trying to make sense of the world in front of her face.

Or the history, the story of it, after it has shed her body.

Silhouette of it in flight.

Debris
Language is always an abbreviation

Debris
Now language is in the land

Debris
Language is a skin

Let yourself be absorbed by the crime. It cannot be sudden.

There is a period between conception and birth in which I was unable to reach you, this is similar. An experience.

An experience connected to fire.

I read most insects begin to lay their eggs soon after fecundation has taken place. She was unable to come back to me. This carriage where blindness and light meet.

I have a sister and my sister became my country.

Hungarian   &   English   Gesture

That we shared the same clothes.

That we shared a name.

That we shared a room.

That we shared a bed.

That we shared a desk at school.

That we went to the bathroom together.

That we showered together.

That we knew each other.

That we were strangers.

That we shared a lanugage.

That we did not share a language.

That we shared a body.

That we did not share a body.

As A

Of A

In A

Essay   on   Sisterhood

In radio talks for the Canadian Broadcasting Company in 1977 (published as "Myth and Meaning: Cracking the Code of Culture"), Mr. Lévi-Strauss demonstrated how a structural examination of myth might proceed. He cited a report that in 17th-century Peru, when the weather became exceedingly cold, a priest would summon all those who had been born feet first, or who had a harelip, or who were twins. They were accused of being responsible for the weather and were ordered to repent, to correct the aberrations. But why these groups? Why harelips and twins?

Mr. Lévi-Strauss cited a series of North American myths that associate twins with opposing natural forces: threat and promise, danger and expectation. One myth, for example, includes a magical hare, a rabbit, whose nose is split in a fight, resulting, literally, in a harelip, suggesting an incipient twinness. With his injunctions, the Peruvian priest seemed aware of associations between cosmic disorder and the latent powers of twins.

The New York Times, November 3, 2009

Spoken as pasture
    sky broken earth

           a groan in the growing

reflection,
how two lungs resemble

              a roof

        possibility re-assembling
    interruption, an interrogation

hold yourself up to this light

Essay   on   Sisterhood

Your sister is an antinomian. She was raised by wolves in the 16th century. She was raised in communist Hungary. You don't know much about the experience of communism. You like the color red. You read a book about it once. Certain words or references or premonitions were thrown from the mouth and burned. You do not like the idea of mouths burning. For your sister this was not an idea.

No matter how sturdy a house
is always pointing up

        a trail in each splintered tile's

           legible roof scratched over
           as branches scratch the blank sky

        now structured here

    among these passages
    sky held inside as breath

        to utter, hunch, shrill, pour, or speak
        hordes of it, rising home

Essay   on   Sisterhood

Human space is a cohabitation with fog. Our clothes are damp with it. Every sort of illuminated depth is astonishing. I have seen the burrow inside my own eye. Nature expanded into a premonition that the world is reincarnated. The essence of the brown and green color captures the process. Christopher Columbus did not voyage in the name of a country, but of an idea. The subject matter of this is obsession. You and I are in a relationship. We are glistening with what it evokes.

Every gullet is a composition,
a wooden pasture of light

and learns to breed wild confrontation

mouth is also round, subject to vocalized wilderness
each circumference

bringing forth to reside

our remain,

a residual herd

Essay   on   Sisterhood

Weather is just one example. But this is exaggerated. Her tone was not one of implication. She was gesturing to have a body.

The clouds did not move. The birds did not fly. No tree stirred.

The wind came up. The tide swelled. The disordered clouds rolled along. The seabirds soared. The thickets shook.

Someone was looking at her. What a fine little sister, they said.

Attempting Embrace: A Crisis in Form(ing)

Attempting Embrace: A Crisis in Form(ing)

"One should never see with one's eyes of flesh
The metaphors hidden
In human beings."
—Hélène Cixous, *Rootprints*

Notes from the Body:

What I recognize is that the confrontation with my sister was an amazingly generative and destructive mechanism in my life. I always feel that my attempt at capturing it doesn't do justice to the actual— because it isn't a "story" and shouldn't be one; it was a physical shift, a change in (of) the body. And I know that, but don't know what it means and am not sure how the body remembers or how the body tells, except that maybe it essays (attempts).

two languages coming into direct contact

And then I spoke and what I said was no longer comprehended. And then she spoke and I found a lack where moments before there had been meaning. This is the awakening of the eyes. A world of images and voicelessness. In that year my voice box receded into my body, an extra layer of muscle burying it inside my throat. The new difficulty of speaking loudly, of speaking at all. Our first conversation was performed by the body. An electrical charge, the light of sentences. An encounter. Martin Buber writes, "When two people relate to each other authentically and humanly, God is the electricity that surges between them." A streak of light between our edges. It's true I could no longer say the word "I," to bear meaning. I flat-lined into "beyond the body," a darkness spreading, darkness gaining shape and I saw, the pupil of my eye forming, and then I saw her black hair.

the body does not have the same ideas that I have

Goulish, Matthew. *39 Microlectures in Proximity of Performance.* New York: Routledge, 2000.

> "My body is not mine.
> My body is not me.
> My body is not my Self" (78).

". . . Performance, like dreaming, presents us with intersections. In a performance, a performer is not a single entity. Instead of a unit, a performer is an identity in motion in a particular direction. A performer is a BECOMING" (78).

Deleuze, Gilles, and Felix Guattari. *A Thousand Plateaus: Capitalism & Schizophrenia.* Trans. Brian Massumi. New York: Continuum, 1987.

"Becoming is a rhizome, not a classificatory or genealogical tree. Becoming is certainly not imitating, or identifying with something; neither is it regressing-progressing; neither is it corresponding, establishing corresponding relations; neither is it producing, producing a filiation or producing through filiation. Becoming is a verb with a consistency all its own; it does not reduce to, or lead back to, 'appearing,' 'being,' 'equaling,' or 'producing' " (239).

Notes on Performance:

In Lin Hixson's *Durations* course at The School of the Art Institute of Chicago, we would perform exercises similar to those I've performed as a writer, in writing classes. The difference being, when the body is presented with a prompt, the body answers (before a sentence is formed by the voice). The body forms its own sentence that is not recognized by the voice, or by language. It is later, at night when I am writing, that I am surprised to find a sentence that is itself a translation of this (earlier) act of the body.

One of the performances I created for that class (under the constraint of a duration of 10 minutes) was a series of still movements taken from Muybridge's photos of the human body. I would pose as one of the stills for one minute (counting out this minute in my mind) and then turn, into the next still (repeating my count). I wore a blindfold during the rehearsal of the performance to experience how I would be affected when I was not able to see the audience. Counting out each minute took a great deal of concentration. I could think about nothing but the unit of time and what number I was on in my count. No longer being able to see away from myself, I found I was able to become the sentence my body was making. A sentence and a performance as a period of time.

Notes on AND / DNA:

One of my investigations for the Andrea/Andrea project is how the word *and* influences us. What does it mean for the word *and* to exist in the world, in language? How does it affect our relationships to one another; how does it double? One of my other investigations is heredity and through it DNA (as a motion or appearance of coming together and moving apart, i.e., attempting embrace). Somehow it took me months to see that these two words are the same; they share the same body.

Notes from Other Bodies:

Cooley, Nicole. "Painful Bodies: Kathy Acker's Last Texts." *We Who Love to Be Astonished: Experimental Women's Writing and Performance Poetics.* Ed. Laura Hinton and Cynthia Hogue. London: The University of Alabama Press, 2002.

"As in *Eurydice in the Underworld*, the experience of the suffering body can only be experienced by the autobiographical subject as a performance, a series of gestures or acts that the body takes on" (199).

". . . Acker wants to believe that writing can make the body a site of resistance, that writing can save the body . . . she wants to heal herself, as if she might write a textual body that could become her material body" (202).

". . . a body of work that explores the work of the body" (202).

Frost, Elisabeth A. "In Another Tongue: Body, Image, Text in Theresa Hak Kyung Cha's *Dictée*." *We Who Love to Be Astonished: Experimental Women's Writing and Performance Poetics.* Ed. Laura Hinton and Cynthia Hogue. London: The University of Alabama Press, 2002.

". . . all translation is only a somewhat provisional way of coming to terms with the foreignness of languages" (189).

"*Dictée* raises the possibility of a 'bothness' of word and flesh that might negotiate between the empirical body and the constructed body, transparency and opacity, original and translation. The tongue becomes a figure for such a border zone: forger of words, organ at the boundary of the body and the symbolic, the tongue retains a stubborn corporeality (more pronounced, for example, than that of the eyes, figured as transcendent 'soul')" (189).

". . . the 'you' is positioned in an impossible space, in which physical location has dissolved and the shattered subject struggles to keep the body whole" (191).

A loss of tongue = a loss of home.

There had already been a loss of location. An orphaning in the space of the home. A birding as I flew / migrating from one state to another and back and back and back. The replacement of voice, of name, of cultural mother is more than a slap in the face; it was an undoing. We felt it as our ribs unfolded, a betrayal in the genome, this new collision with open air. To become this monstrous body, my sister Andrea and I found two options, to invent new forms, or to strip the current one; to strip it, then shoot it up with heroin.

I was the heron. She was the heroine, of course.

Sister Sutures

Sister Sutures

I wore my white dress into tattering. Quality thus expressed as
expressionless.
Indent hit margin, margin. Release. I let my
hem down I let her touch my white space.

She held my scaffolding in her hand she held my broader border. Her
ship makes passage between continent and continent.

I love where she is Australia and wince
in the margin where we index how freckle on her neck meant place to
take port
and for me bridge between the eyes is an ocean / area.

What shall we name her
Arctic.

No name her Atlas no name her
Atlast.

History   of   Sewing

The needle was modeled on the shape of the bird's beak and the sewing-machine, its hesitations. Diagrams of bird migration reveal flight as a form of stitching. Path an attempt at binding oneself to specific location. Flight a bird makes across the sky. The bird has a magnet huddled in its blood to give thread direction. ^^^^^^^^^^^^. Gathering fabric, elements, into circumference is a motion of gravity, then of ascension. This movement resembles the hem, to drag a line above ground, then back below ground.

The body has been said to mimic the act of sewing. In *The Symposium* Aristophanes defines love as an impulse that has its impetus in our constant search for a second half. This half was once sewn to the back of us.

Surface and dive down

what rising up erasing

relation no relation

I am the deer small noun

in the forest

finite and of the waves

crowd me in my face

and the leaves, leave

me to fashion myself

Envelope / Hem

In the distance some small figure is wielding us self. Who we are will be met with light. The woman removes an egg.   .from her it is made.   .enamel and motion.   .this is true.   .have faith.

Faith. My fate speaks of. In the dark my name fades. Remains.

where seams surface in me.   .describing what is inside.   .what is white.   .the self is surface lined.   .a broad seam stitch.   .carrying over to place.   .what surface gathered at said edges gathered a name, a named place.

Earth strikes the roof of my mouth; letters it certain part.
A stray scripture spoken. Faith does not act upon the body, as pulpit.
Is what gravity is; the voice in the vowel.

Certain parts of the body inhabit the world.
Teeth bite and bare the tongue, hemming the tongue to its home.

To be, to be made and structured. To be hollowed out and felled in. And ever on the brink of furthering, on the brink of rapture. To rupture. To toil and burn in the echo. To envelop. To breathe in and hold as landscape. To lunge. To lean against the edge becoming. To pin a map and all its edgeless swarming body. To swarm again and whole.

Here will I spell me out
the world
shucked from my own skin

the whorled
fields a corresponding

portion of bone, *exegesis*

I am framed.

My life in this band of hemisphere

the edge an endless dwelling
exhales and moves back into my temple

History   of   Reading   as   Stitching

To recall that each movement is an inquiry. That Eden is our
wilderness now. Divided as it is doubled. A path marked with
contradictions, with the word *refrain*. To repeat, or to hold back.
Every remove should correspond to a passage. It is how we know
who we are. Mary Rowlandson ate raw meat and blood ran down the
edges of her mouth. Dickinson a manifestation of this same
uncertainty. To shut the door more fully. She stitched her poems
into pamphlets. One's physical location locked away. One's body
becoming less necessary, or more so. Dressed in white blank paper.
Teach us how to read. Mary Rowlandson wrote the word *salvage*
inside her dressing gown. She ate the fetus of a deer. What does
redemption mean.

Selvedge

Myself set sail

claims reunite me

recompense

for all that is past

our undoing

at the seam.

I see me as one

or more, or both

of me I know, the rift

the body cannot say

I cannot stay this body.

The body cannot stay

governed, cannot

dissipate known regions

to become renowned

to become owned noun

my name adheres

to trace an outline

subjects itself

upon the white

of the eye.

Of the eye is

a map I am wearing,

twenty-first century neon

gown of the ground

gone, the world

a dress

is the only address

I know.

The only address I know is yes

and yet again is yes.

History   of   Reading   as   Stitching

We have invented how the world gets caught. A pattern of lines allow us to read the identity of a person as it is inscribed on their body. Our literacy is partial. It is genetic, as in a strand of DNA, or a strand of hair.

To stitch: to pull something together in context, to combine two unlike things in association. A stitch as metaphor, the near and far touching tentatively. A temporary outpouring of relationship. As long as the stitch will hold.

Gravity / Hem

Ground is beast. It breathes
beneath me. Its mouth a cave
as my own formed from dirt.
A cove. Water running into it,
then a roof.

A chapel. Images carved onto palate
holding flight, swallows back refrain.
All the gone words a swallow. A white
thread to pull knot from throat. A light
to pull from ground. Now bitten, now
blackened, root.

Earth is a tree branch held at bay
from its body. A restraint of gravity.
All drinking moves up the trunk throat.
Follicles bend back tell sun they have seen it.
In winter, all returns to hearth.

Ground an exit.
Sound as seed
grown in heat.
Moisture.

A tongue, in the anthole. How breathing occurs.
The horizon is just the edge of my own mouth;
billowed. The heart carries gills. An animal buried
in deep water where unknown light hits.

The ground. The entryway of heat.
A forecast, light scatters.

Where earth is severed. Trunk of a tree.
Light dwells upon it. A heart in rotten
wood. A tongue an overgrown weed. Light
heals. And hears ground's response. Each
carries each root and names it. Dogwood;
a bite mark in grass.

A tunnel has been dug. Another opening
forming. Tell tale of water rustling
like leaves outside a window. Curtain is
drawn but light is still there. Voice makes
thread in mouth a little nest too.

Ground. A little nest of light.
A mouth of light. A mouth a moth
to light. In the chapel
there is a roof.

Hunted deer in cheek.
Of a chapel, of its roof.
A pasture. Hoof print in mouth.
Of dirt, to taste. Placed root,
a tree branch here.

Heart its own animal. Alive
as eye as tongue. A breathing lamp.
A chord to tug on to alter circuit.

Made of dirt a seed distinguishes
shape. Beholds water as tendril
stalk; a stitch. Ground is floor, a
roof. A hole in it.

History   of   Human   Dissection

Etymology traces slight changes in pronunciation of a word over time. These are not inundations. Their travel marks an erosion, as in saliva wearing the basin of the mouth away. A single river is never the same river, a word never the same, having traveled as water over the lungs. If I repeat *selvedge, selvedge, selvedge* you may begin to notice it consists of two words conjoined. Invention of the selvedge is concordant with recognition of the self. Distinction is the beginning of dissection.

Friction

The move is always more powerful than the thing moved. Cause of swallowing. Cause of coughing. Cause of the numbness of various limbs. Cause of the tickling sensation. Cause of sensuality and other necessities of the body. Cause of urination. Cause of the sense of touch. See how birds are nourished in their eggs. See how muscles grasp the opening of the lung. Remedy is a decoction of red chick peas, of asparagus in a fine powder. Mingled together and consumed by a dilation of fibers.

NOTES:

All photos are of Joan & Jean Hedstrom, the author's grandmother and her twin.

The quote on page 6 is from Tomkins, Silvan S. *Affect Imagery Consciousness*. 4 vols. New York: Springer, 1962-1992.

Sections from page 86 and the quote on page 5 are from Leonardo Di Vinci's *Notebooks*, republished by Dover in 1983 (p. 118).

Sections on page 40 are from Kasulis, Thomas P., Roger T. Aimes, and Wimal Dissanayake. *Self as body in Asian Theory and Practice*. New York: SUNY Press, 1993 (p. 271).

My apologies to my half-brother, Ben, for temporarily denying his existance on page 3 of this book.

ACKNOWLEDGEMENTS:

Thank you to the editors of the following journals for publishing versions of this work: *A Plod*, *Bird Dog*, *Court Green*, *Dritto*, *Minor American*, *Octopus*, *OR*, *Play/No Play*, and to Jen Tynes and Horse Less Press for publishing a large section of this as a chapbook, and to Caryl Pagel and Danny Khalastchi for all of their efforts in putting together this book. I appreciate the support and feedback of all of my classmates and teachers at SAIC and DU, but most especially, Bin Ramke, Eleni Sikelianos, Selah Saterstrom, Dan Beachy-Quick, Eric Baus, Della Watson, and Olivia Cronk.

BIOGRAPHY:

Andrea Rexilius completed her Ph.D. in Literature and Writing at the University of Denver. She is co-editor of Marcel Press. Her second book, *Half Of What They Carried Flew Away*, is forthcoming from Letter Machine Editions.

RESCUE
+PRESS